EXPLORE BIOMES

FRESHWATER BIOMES

BY CECILIA PINTO McCARTHY

Kids Core
An Imprint of Abdo Publishing
abdobooks.com

abdobooks.com

Published by Abdo Publishing, a division of ABDO, PO Box 398166, Minneapolis, Minnesota 55439. Copyright © 2024 by Abdo Consulting Group, Inc. International copyrights reserved in all countries. No part of this book may be reproduced in any form without written permission from the publisher. Kids Core™ is a trademark and logo of Abdo Publishing.

Printed in the United States of America, North Mankato, Minnesota.
052023
092023

THIS BOOK CONTAINS RECYCLED MATERIALS

Cover Photo: Shutterstock Images
Interior Photos: Karl R. Martin/Shutterstock Images, 4–5; iStockphoto, 6; Matt Anderson/iStockphoto, 8; Niwat Panket/Shutterstock Images, 10–11; Ody Stocker/Shutterstock Images, 13; Shutterstock Images, 14, 16, 18–19, 23, 28 (duck); Nadezhda Kharitonova/Shutterstock Images, 21; Brian Lasenby/iStockphoto, 24; Cathy Keifer/Shutterstock Images, 26; Suriyo Tataisong/Shutterstock Images, 28 (frog); Kazakova Maryia/Shutterstock Images, 28–29 (background)

Editor: Angela Lim
Series Designer: Ryan Gale

Library of Congress Control Number: 2022949085

Publisher's Cataloging-in-Publication Data

Names: McCarthy, Cecilia Pinto, author.
Title: Freshwater biomes / by Cecilia Pinto McCarthy
Description: Minneapolis, Minnesota: Abdo Publishing Company, 2024 | Series: Explore biomes | Includes online resources and index.
Identifiers: ISBN 9781098291099 (lib. bdg.) | ISBN 9781098277277 (ebook)
Subjects: LCSH: Rivers--Juvenile literature. | Biotic communities--Juvenile literature. | Habitats--Juvenile literature. | Life zones--Juvenile literature. | Stream animals--Juvenile literature. | Stream plants--Juvenile literature. | Stream ecology--Juvenile literature.
Classification: DDC 577--dc23

CONTENTS

CHAPTER 1
Going Fishing 4

CHAPTER 2
How Freshwater Biomes Form 10

CHAPTER 3
Life in Freshwater Biomes 18

Explore the Biome 28
Glossary 30
Online Resources 31
Learn More 31
Index 32
About the Author 32

Great blue herons live in freshwater biomes such as marshes and swamps.

GOING FISHING

A great blue heron stands on its long legs in the shallow water of a pond. The heron waits near some cattail plants. It stretches its neck and holds still. It focuses on the water. The heron is watching for movement.

Cattails are typically found in marshes and shallow regions of ponds and lakes.

Suddenly ripples appear on the water's surface. The heron jabs its beak into the water. It pulls up a sunfish. The hungry bird flips its head up and swallows the fish whole.

What Is a Freshwater Biome?

Earth is made up of biomes. A biome is a large area that includes certain types of animals, plants, and nonliving things. **Climate** affects the living things in a biome. Herons and sunfish are freshwater animals. Cattails are freshwater plants. Nonliving things such as water and rocks are also part of the biome.

Rivers, streams, lakes, ponds, and wetlands are all made up of fresh water. Rivers and streams have water that flows in one direction. Lakes, ponds, and wetlands have standing water that does not move much.

A Rich Biome

Freshwater biomes are made up of a rich variety of life. There are more than 140,000 freshwater species worldwide. This includes approximately 18,000 kinds of fish, 560 types of birds, and 30,000 species of plants.

Many people rely on rivers for fresh drinking water.

Fresh water is less than 1 percent salt. Only 3 percent of the water on Earth is fresh water. Much of it is frozen at the North and South Poles. Freshwater biomes are not just important for the plants and animals that live there. People need fresh water too. They depend on freshwater biomes for water to drink and to help grow crops.

PRIMARY SOURCE

The World Wildlife Fund describes how rare fresh water is:

> Water covers 70 percent of our planet. . . . However, fresh water . . . is incredibly rare. . . . As a result, some 1.1 billion people worldwide lack access to water, and a total of 2.7 billion find water [rare] for at least one month of the year.

Source: "Water Scarcity." *World Wildlife Fund*, n.d., wwf.org. Accessed 12 Aug. 2022.

Comparing Texts

Think about the quote. Does it support the information in this chapter? What new information did you learn?

Hot Springs National Park in Arkansas has 47 natural hot springs.

CHAPTER 2

HOW FRESHWATER BIOMES FORM

Precipitation brings water to freshwater biomes. Some water collects underground in areas called aquifers and becomes groundwater. Groundwater forms some freshwater biomes. It comes to the surface through springs.

Glaciers also provide water for some freshwater biomes. They melt and form streams and rivers. Glaciers can also carve out **basins**. They fill the basins with water as they melt.

Streams and Rivers

Streams tend to be smaller and shallower than rivers. They are also narrower. Streams may combine and form a river. Some streams and rivers flow into lakes or oceans. Or they may dry out before reaching another body of water.

Some rivers flow quickly. Other rivers have slow **currents**. Rivers pick up soil and rocks as they flow. This can change the color of the river. Bits of soil make the Yellow River in China a yellowish-brown color.

The Water Cycle

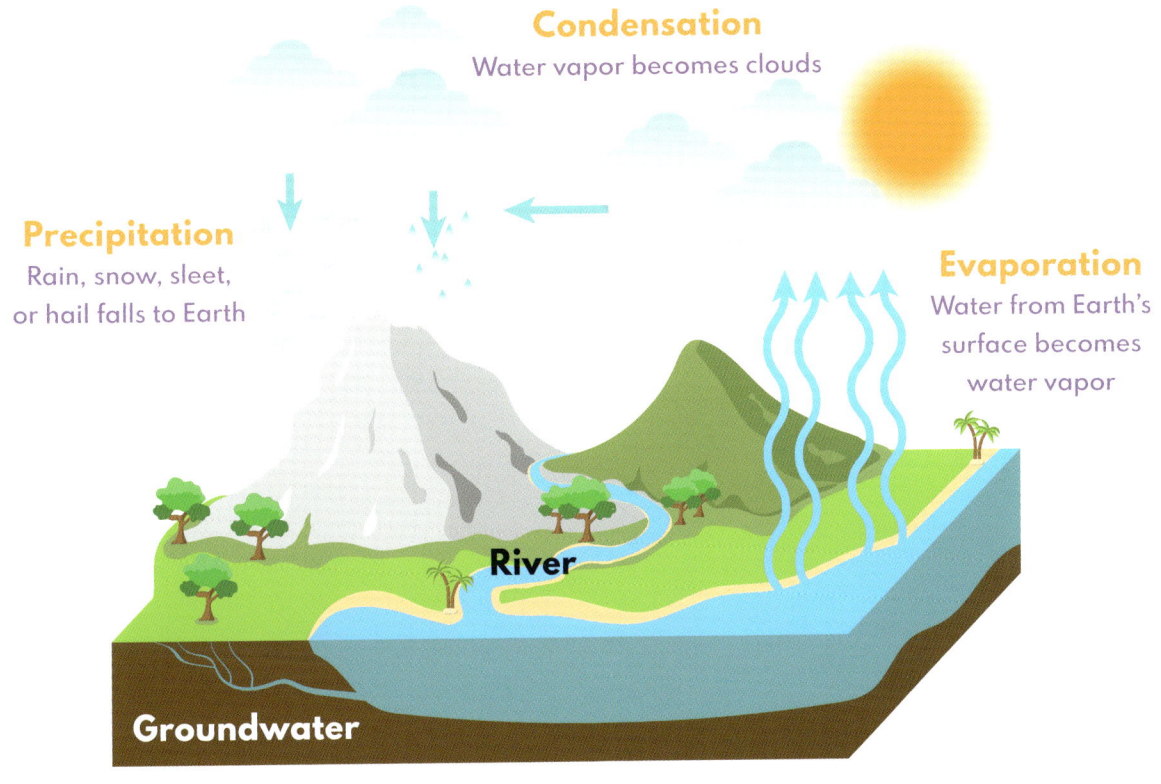

The water cycle maintains freshwater biomes and groundwater. Precipitation and groundwater form rivers, lakes, and other bodies of water.

Ponds and Lakes

Lakes and ponds can be divided into layers.

Deep layers get less sunlight than the surface.

A melting glacier formed Peyto Lake, which is in Banff National Park in Canada.

They are also colder. Some plants and animals are found only at certain depths.

Lakes are larger and deeper than ponds. Sunlight cannot reach the bottom of some lakes.

Because ponds are shallow, plants get enough sunlight to grow at the bottom. Shallow ponds may freeze completely in the winter. Only water close to the surface of deep lakes freezes.

Wetlands

Shallow standing water covers the ground in wetlands most or all of the year.

Bubbles on Lake Baikal

Matter at the bottom of Lake Baikal in Russia releases a gas called methane. The gas rises to the surface of the lake in bubbles. During the winter, these bubbles freeze as they near the surface. People from around the world come to see the frozen bubbles of Lake Baikal.

Water lilies are common plants in wetlands.

Groundwater forms some wetlands. Others are located near bodies of water.

Swamps, marshes, and bogs are types of wetlands. Wetlands have different types of plants and soils. Swamps and marshes have soils that are rich in **nutrients**. Trees can grow in swamps. Marshes tend to have only grasses and reeds. The soil in bogs does not have many nutrients. Bogs support plants such as mosses and small shrubs.

The Pantanal in South America is the largest wetland system in the world. It covers approximately 68,000 square miles (176,119 sq km). The Pantanal includes swamps and marshes.

> ### Further Evidence
> Look at the website below. What evidence does it give to support Chapter Two?
>
> ### Wetland
> abdocorelibrary.com/freshwater-biomes

Animals such as crocodiles live in swamps and marshes.

CHAPTER **3**

LIFE IN FRESHWATER BIOMES

Certain plants and animals are **adapted** to life in fresh water. They have traits that help them thrive in their environments. Freshwater plants and animals interact with each other.

Freshwater Plants

Plants can live in different depths of water. They can live in standing or moving water. Duckweed prefers standing water. It grows at the surface. Many ducks and fish eat duckweed.

Tape grass grows entirely underwater. It does not need much sunlight. The roots anchor the plants to the bottom of the lake or pond. Fish and insects hide in tape grass. They eat the leaves. Manatees eat tape grass too.

Venus flytraps and pitcher plants grow in bogs. Because bogs don't have many nutrients, these two plants trap and digest insects for nutrients. Cranberries and blueberries also grow in bogs.

Venus flytraps digest flies, beetles, and sometimes small frogs.

Animal Life

Many animals thrive in the world's freshwater biomes. Most catfish and sturgeon are freshwater fish. These fish have special whiskers called barbels. Barbels have taste buds. Catfish and sturgeon drag their barbels on the bottoms of lakes and rivers to find food.

Dragonflies and mosquitoes are insects that live in freshwater biomes. They lay their eggs in water. The young hatch and live underwater. They fly above water as adults. These insects and many others are food sources for other animals.

Frogs spend much of their lives in or around fresh water. They lay their eggs in ponds and streams. Tadpoles hatch from the eggs. They eat

Catfish usually live at the bottom of a body of water.

freshwater plants and algae. The adult frogs can survive on land.

Freshwater biomes are also home to waterbirds. The common loon has webbed feet that help it dive. It spears fish with its sharp beak.

Common loons have black-and-white patterned feathers during the summer.

Beavers are another freshwater animal. They cut down trees with their teeth. They use branches to build dams across waterways.

Dams block the flow of water. They create shallow ponds where beavers raise their young.

Freshwater biomes are rich with plant and animal life. But these biomes are in danger. Pollution from cities runs off into waterways. And people drain wetlands to plant crops.

Dams and Ladders

People build dams to control water flow. The water held back by dams can be used as drinking water. But dams can be harmful to wildlife. Some salmon swim up rivers to lay eggs. Dams make it difficult for the fish to reach their **breeding grounds**. People can add fish ladders to dams. These are a series of shallow pools that salmon can jump between. The ladders give the salmon a way to get over the dam.

Freshwater biomes are made up of many types of plants and animals.

A changing climate also adds stress to these biomes. Increasing temperatures affect the survival of plants and animals. People are working to protect these natural areas.

Explore Online

Visit the website below. Does it give any new information about freshwater plants and animals that wasn't in Chapter Three?

Freshwater

abdocorelibrary.com/freshwater-biomes

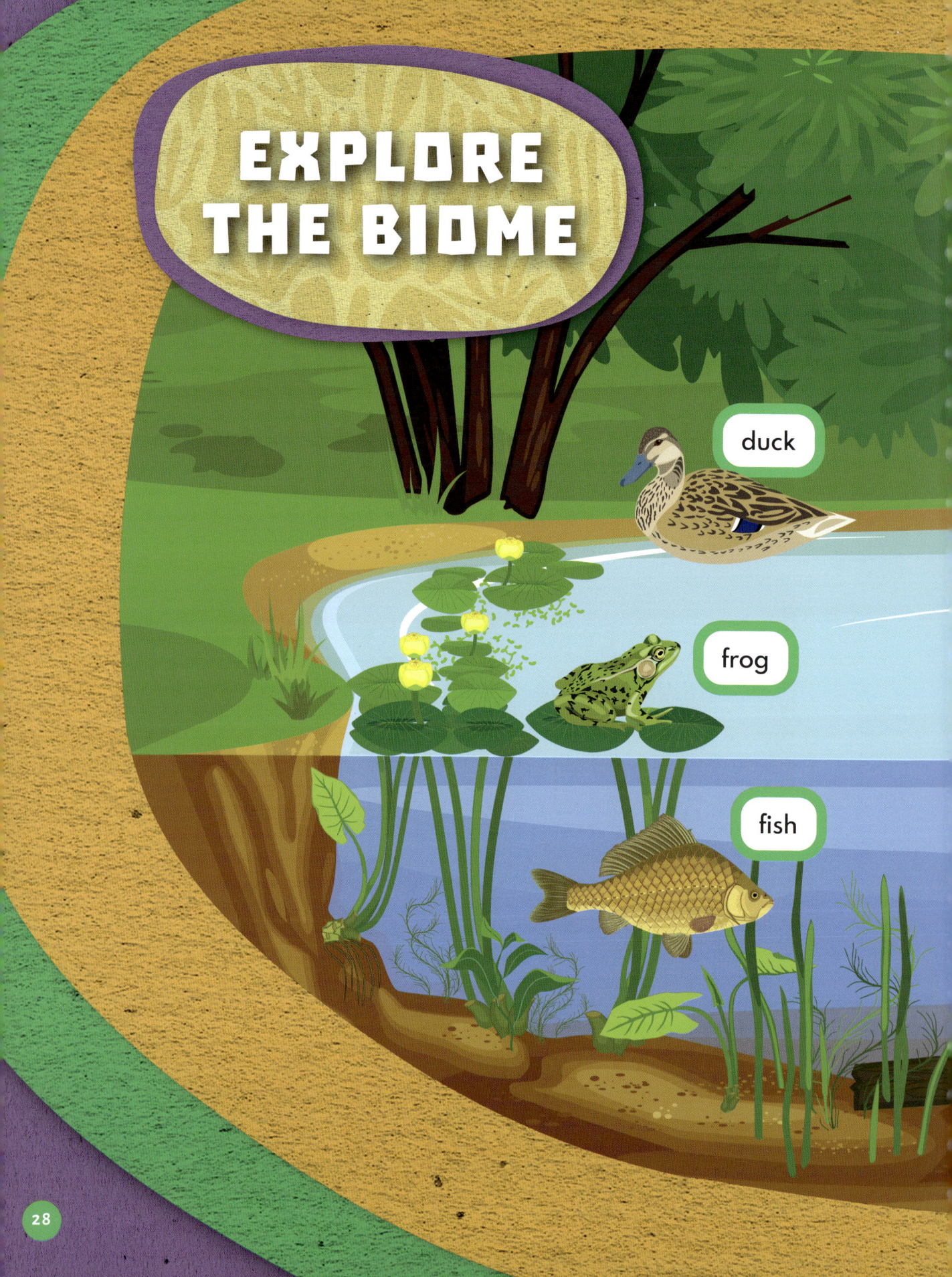

Glossary

adapted
adjusted to survive in a certain biome

basins
low areas of land

breeding grounds
areas where animals go to mate and give birth

climate
the weather conditions in an area over time

currents
the flow or movements of water

glaciers
large bodies of snow and ice that move across land

nutrients
materials that living things need in order to grow and stay alive

precipitation
liquid or frozen water that falls from the sky, including rain, sleet, and snow

Online Resources

To learn more about freshwater biomes, visit our free resource websites below.

Visit **abdocorelibrary.com** or scan this QR code for free Common Core resources for teachers and students, including vetted activities, multimedia, and booklinks, for deeper subject comprehension.

Visit **abdobooklinks.com** or scan this QR code for free additional online weblinks for further learning. These links are routinely monitored and updated to provide the most current information available.

Learn More

Bender, Douglas. *Ponds*. Crabtree, 2022.

Huddleston, Emma. *Food Chains*. Abdo, 2022.

London, Martha. *Ecosystems*. Abdo, 2022.

Index

beavers, 24–25
bogs, 16–17, 20

cattails, 5, 7

duckweed, 20

fish, 6–7, 20, 22–23, 25
frogs, 22–23

glaciers, 12
great blue herons, 5–7
groundwater, 11, 13, 16

insects, 20, 22

lakes, 7, 12–15, 20, 22

ponds, 5, 7, 13–15, 20, 22, 25

rivers, 7, 12, 13, 22, 25

streams, 7, 12, 22

tape grass, 20

wetlands, 7, 15–17, 25

About the Author

Cecilia Pinto McCarthy enjoys sharing her love of nature with young readers. When she is not writing, she teaches at a nature center. She lives north of Boston, Massachusetts.